My Accented
Bilingual Book
of
IGBO &
ENGLISH
Words

Helena Chinweoke

Paperback ISBN: 978-1-7376021-0-1
Hardcover ISBN: 978-1-7376021-1-8
Ebook ISBN: 978-1-7376021-2-5

Published & Illustrated By Opportune Independent Publishing Company

Printed in the United States of America

For permission requests, email the publisher with the subject line as "Attention: Permissions Coordinator" to the email address below.

info@opportunepublishing.com
www. opportunepublishing.com

Acknowledgments

This book celebrates and encourages people all over the world to embrace and promulgate the beautiful Igbo culture regardless of where they are or come from. It is dedicated to my parents Sebastian & Ann Eke who raised me to know my roots. I appreciate my siblings, family and friends who encourage me to never give up. Special shout out to Rakesh K. and Amna for helping me with this!

PEOPLE

Husband and Wife
Dí nà Nwúnyè

Twins
Èjìmá

Sibling
Nwánné

Woman
Nwányì

Man
Nwókē

Friend
Ényì

Elderly Person
Ágádī

Young Man
Òkórọ̀bìà

Photographer
Ónyé fòtó

Young lady
Àgbọ́ghọbìà

Child
Nwá

Priest
Ụ́kọ̀chúkwú

PLACES

Hospital
Ụ́lọ̀ ọ́gwụ̀

Hill
Úgwú

University
Máhādùm

School
Ụ́lọ̀ ákwụ́kwọ́

Government House
Òbí Gọ́ọ́méntì

Market
Áhị́á

Playground
Ámá Égwùrégwū

Forest
Óké ọ́hị́á

Church
Ụ́lọ̀ úkà

TRANSPORT

Airplane
Úgbọ́ élū

Boat
Úgbọ́ mmìrì

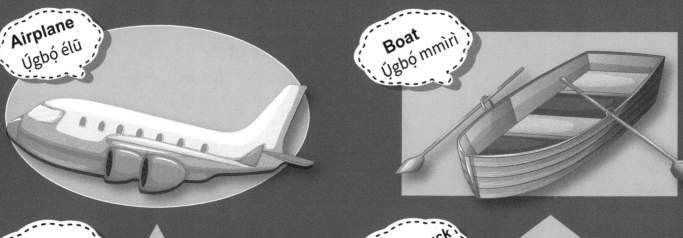

Car
Úgbọ́ Àlà

Lorry\Truck
Gwóngwórò

Motorcycle
Ògbátùmtùm

Bicycle
Ànyìnyà ígwè

PARTS OF BODY

HAIR Ntùtù	**HEAD** Ísí
EYE Ányá	**Face** Írú
NOSE Ímí	**TEETH** Ézē
EAR Ntị	**MOUTH** Ọnụ́
CHEEK Ǹtì	**TONGUE** Íré
CHIN Àgbà	**Armpit** Ábụ̀
HANDS Áká	**STOMACH** Áfọ́
FINGERS Mkpị sị́ákā	**NAILS** Mbọ́
BACK Àzụ́	**BELLYBUTTON** Ótùbò
KNEE Íkpèrè	**LEGS** Ụ́kwụ́
FOOT Ọ́kpà	**FINGERnails** Mbọ́ ákā
TOES Mkpị sị́ ụ́kwụ̀	**Toenails** Mbọ́ ụ́kwụ̀

KITCHEN

Salt
Ńnú

pepper
Ósè

Salt

Pepper

Basket
Nkàtà

Sponge
Ògbó

Pot cover
Ókwúchí ìtè

Soap
Nchà

P
Ìt

Water
Mmírī

Small Mortar
Ọ́kwá

Cup
ìkọ́

Chair
Óché

Flowers
Òkóòkò/Ífùrù

FOODS

Rice
Òsìkápá

Eggs
Àkwá

Pepper
Ósè

Beans
Àgwà

Bread
Àchịchà

Corn
Ọ́kà

Pumpkin
Ányụ́

Plantains
Ògèdè

Honey
Mmánụ́ ányụ

Cassava
Ákpụ́

Yam
Jí

Cocoyam
Édè

Onions
Yàbásị

Meat
Ánụ́

Okra
Ọ́kwụ̀rụ̀

FRUITS & NUTS

Banana
Únèrè

Orange
Òròmá

Lime
Òròmá
Nkírísí

Pawpaw
Ọ̀kwùrù
Bekee

Mango
Mángòrò

Water melon
Ányụ́ mmírị

Guava
Goova

African Star Apple
Ụ́dárà

Coconut
Ákụ́ Óyìbó

Palmnuts
Ákụ́/ Ákị́

Bitter kola
Ákị́ ínū

Pepper fruit
Mmìmì

Velvet tamarind
Ìchékū

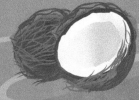

Peanuts
Áhúékérē

Kola nut
Ọ́jị̄

MUSICAL INSTRUMENTS

Metal gong
Ògénè

Elephant tusk horn
Ọ́dụ́

Wooden xylophone
Ìkpà/Ògè

Long metal gong
Áló

Bell
Mgbịrịmgbá

Small horn
Ọ́dụ́ mkpáló

Double-horned metal gong
Ògénè Mkpị Àbụ́ọ́

Basket rattle
ọ́yọ̀

OCCUPATIONS

Doctor
Díbịà Óyìbó

Chief
Ìchíè

King
Ézè

Queen
Ézè nwányị

Warrior
Díkē ọ̀gụ̀

Farmer
Ọ́nyé ọ́rụ́ úgbọ̀

Chef
Òsí ńrị́

Teacher
Ónyé nkúzí

Police
Ónyé ùwè ójíí

Dancer
ónyé égwū

Student
Nwátà ákwụ́kwọ́

Security Guard
Ónyé ńché

Printed in the USA
CPSIA information can be obtained
at www.ICGtesting.com
LVHW070027291023
762448LV00014B/707